© 2022 by ADISAN Publishing AB, Sweden

No part of this publication may be reproduced, stored in a retrieval system, or transmitted in any form or by any means, electronic, mechanical, photocopying, recording, scanning, or otherwise as permitted under section 107 and 108 of the 1976 United States Copyright Act, without the prior permission of the Publisher.

Picture used in the book cover is purchased as per Depositphotos Standard Licenses agreement for commercial purpose.

The images contained in this book are licensed under Creative Copyright, and every image title, source, URL and Creative Copyright license is mentioned in the Acknowledgement. Covers all 40 images used in this book.

Limit of Liability/ Disclaimer of Warranty: The publisher and the author make no representations or warranties concerning the accuracy or completeness of this work's content and expressly. Neither the Publisher nor the author shall be liable for damages arising here.

Advertisement for Children

.. he deserves the Flash!

Master-designed for lightness, and
with its built-in strength and gleaming
good looks, the FLASH is the machine
that will give your boy the finest
start to his cycling life.

· CENTURYWISE ·
C·W·S
1863-1963

FLASH Model 32

18 in. curved top tube frame. Adult-size
tubing and lugs. 26 in. × 1⅜ in. wheels.
All-rounder handlebars. Sturmey-Archer
3-speed gear. Cable brakes. White wall
tyres. Spring seat saddle. Duo coloured.
Extra long seat pillar allows for wide range
of adjustment. Finish : Lustre Blue or Red.
Extra for Flamboyant finish.

Equipment : Touring Bag, Spanners, Inflator,
Reflector.

£20 · 15 · 0 (inc. P.T.)

C·W·S CYCLES

Ask for H.P. details at your Co-operative Stores

Write for FREE illustrated catalogue to :
C·W·S CYCLE WORKS · KING'S ROAD · BIRMINGHAM 11

Advertisement for Women

BC49D
Ask a Bristol smoker and she'll tell you why Bristol is today's cigarette. Its Multicel tip (so firm, so clean) lets through the full, cool flavour of fine tobacco for the kind of smoking only Bristol smokers know. Just ask a Bristol smoker.
Today's cigarette is a BRISTOL
BRISTOL
TIPPED CIGARETTES
BRISTOL
TIPPED CIGARETTES
FULL SIZE 3/4 FOR 20–1/8 FOR 10

SUNBEAM
SUNBEAM Alpine
SPORTING PERFORMANCE WITH TOURING LUXURY

The
world
swing...

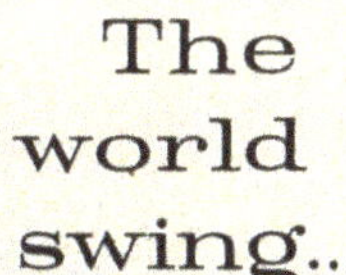

is to
Rothmans
KING SIZE

The world's
largest selling
KING SIZE
virginia
cigarette

Extra tobacco length *plus finer filter*

Priced at 3/11 for 20

In 1951 the Rothman Group introduced their new idea in smoking—KING SIZE FILTER. In that short time smokers have thrown off the habits of over half a century and are switching from old short cigarettes to the modern KING SIZE FILTER which is sweeping the cigarette markets of the world.

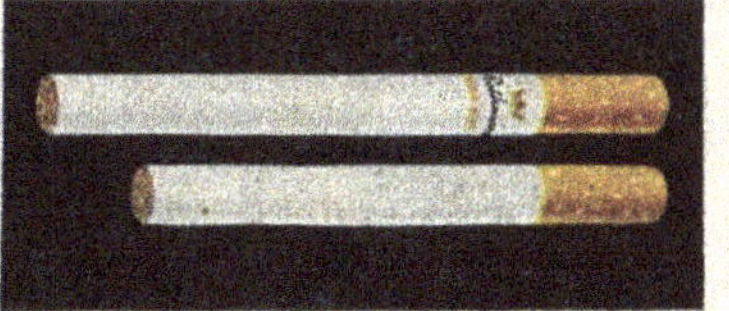

Compare Rothmans King Size Filter—the extra length of best Virginia tobacco plus the *finer* filter gives that *doubly smooth* satisfying flavour.

GREAT BRITAIN · SOUTH AFRICA · CANADA · AUSTRALIA · NEW ZEALAND

Copyright

Music Records (Vinyl release)

BALDWIN MAGIC
GOLDEN MELODIES for easy listening
MOUNTAIN GREENERY
WALTZ OF MY HEART
MAME from "MAME"
I'LL SEE YOU IN MY DREAMS
CHARADE
TOOT TOOT TOOTSIE
BIRTH OF THE BLUES
LA MER
DREAM A LITTLE DREAM
BALI HA'I from "SOUTH PACIFIC"
DANCING FEET
A LOT OF LIVIN' TO DO
featuring VIC HAMMETT at the BALDWIN ORGAN
Sight & Sound of Fine Music
ar
AD-RHYTHM

Music Records (Vinyl release)

Best Cars Of The 60s

Austin/Morris 1100

Best Cars Of The 60s

Vauxhall Victor

Best Cars Of The 60s

Ford Cortina

Top Actors

Sean Connery

Top Actors

Terence Stamp

Top Actresses

Elizabeth Taylor

Top Actresses

Julie Christie

The Beatles

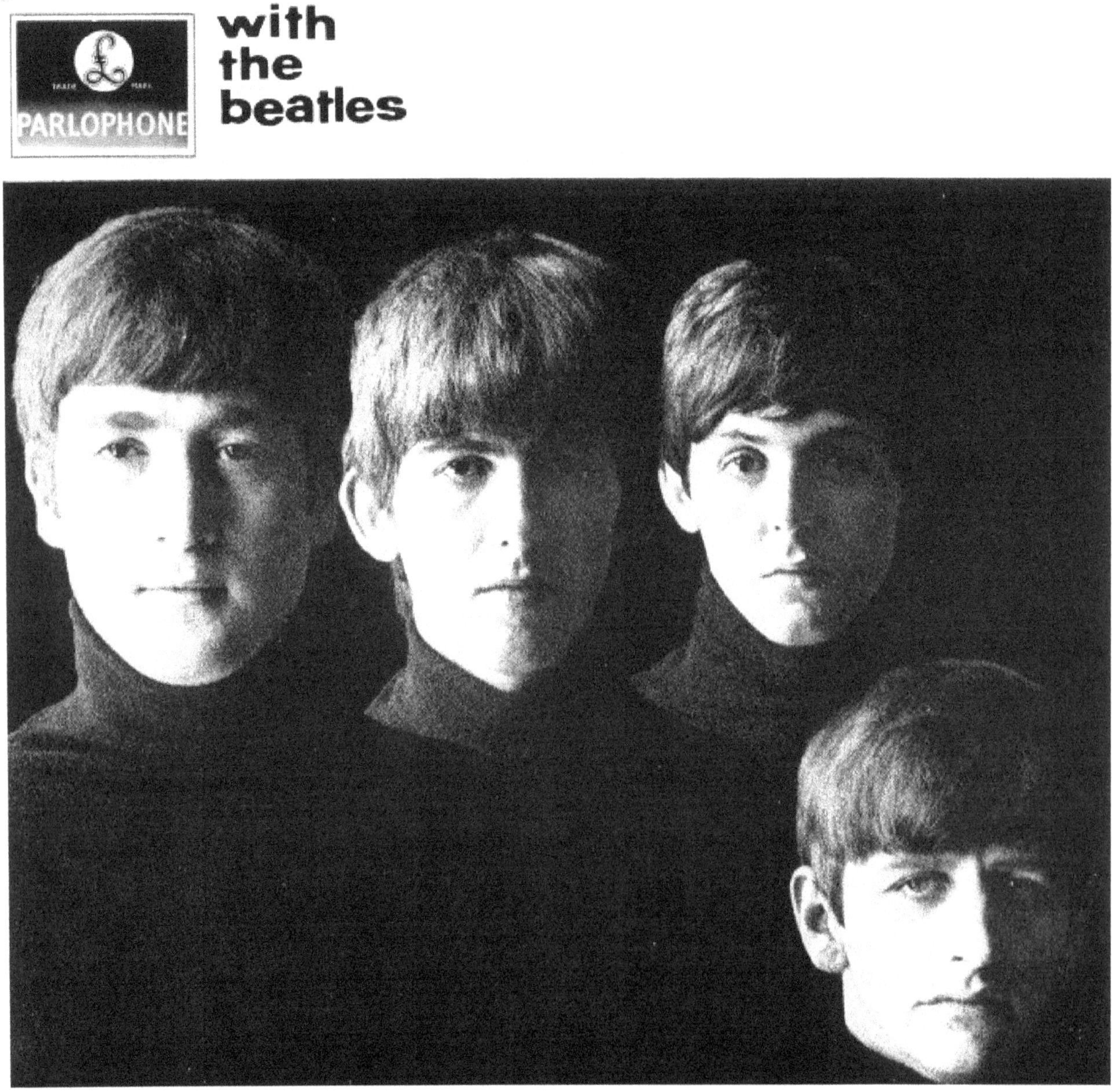

With The Beatles (1963)

The Beatles

Help! (1965)

The Beatles

Abbey Road (1969)

England Wins Football World Cup

First Concorde Flight in 1969

James Bond First Movie (1962)

Ice Lollies

Women's Fashion

Women's Fashion

Women's Fashion

Vintage Post Cards from '60s

Cornwall, 1960s

Vintage Post Cards from '60s

Piccadilly Circus, London 1964

Vintage Post Cards from '60s

Cardiff Castle

Vintage Post Cards from '60s

Hoddesdon postcard, mid 1960s

City Life

Manchester, 1960s

City Life

London, 1960s

Families

Families

Families

School in the 1960s

A MERRY CHRISTMAS TO YOU ALL!
EAGLE
22 December, 1962 Vol. 13 No. 51
EVERY WEDNESDAY
6d.
Across the Atlantic for next to nothing— if you have the NERVE! Meet the man who has already done it three times! See page 16.
18
KINGS OF THE ROAD
Sir Henry Birkin, Bt., driving the supercharged 4½-litre Bentley sports car which won him second place in the 1930 French Grand Prix. (See page 19.)
-CROSS-
© Longacre Press Ltd. England. 1962

British Comics from the 60's

British Comics from the 60's

DAN DARE
PILOT OF THE FUTURE
THE MONOCHROME VOLUME

Acknowledgement

Page No. I Author/s I Title I Source I License

Children Advertisement	Claire	Johnny Astro	https://www.flickr.com/photos/8050359@N07/5288847110/	Attribution 2.0 Generic (CC BY 2.0)
Children Advertisement	Sludge G	CWS Co-operative Flash cycle	https://www.flickr.com/photos/sludgeulper/8377916873/	Attribution-ShareAlike 2.0 Generic (CC BY-SA 2.0)
Advertisement for Women	Sludge G	Queen of the road pram	https://www.flickr.com/photos/sludgeulper/8377918179/	Attribution-ShareAlike 2.0 Generic (CC BY-SA 2.0)
Advertisement for Women	Sludge G	Bristol Tipped Cigarettes	https://www.flickr.com/photos/sludgeulper/4005440807/	Attribution-ShareAlike 2.0 Generic (CC BY-SA 2.0)
Advertisement for Men	ausdew	SUNBEAM ALPINE 1960s	https://www.flickr.com/photos/ausdew/41632328550/	Public Domain
Advertisement for Men	SludgeG	Rothmans King Size advert.	https://www.flickr.com/photos/sludgeulper/4006202858/	Attribution-ShareAlike 2.0 Generic (CC BY-SA 2.0)
Music Records	Mike	Bob Blaine & The Aloha Hawaiians- Hawaiian Honeymoon	https://www.flickr.com/photos/abaraphobia/5011270926/	Attribution-ShareAlike 2.0 Generic (CC BY-SA 2.0)
Music Records	Mike	Vic Hammett at the Baldwin Organ- Baldwin Magic	https://www.flickr.com/photos/abaraphobia/5014335298/	Attribution-ShareAlike 2.0 Generic (CC BY-SA 2.0)
Music Records	Mike	Linda and Noel (Cream)- Your Kind Of Party	https://www.flickr.com/photos/abaraphobia/5011642532/	Attribution-ShareAlike 2.0 Generic (CC BY-SA 2.0)
Top Cars 1960s	Chris Sampson	MUW789D-1 310312 CPS	https://www.flickr.com/photos/lodekka/6902622240/	Attribution-ShareAlike 2.0 Generic (CC BY-SA 2.0)
Top Cars 1960s	Alden Jewell	1960 Vauxhall Victor (U.S. Postcard)	https://www.flickr.com/photos/autohistorian/51828051358/	Attribution 2.0 Generic (CC BY 2.0)
Top Cars 1960s	Alden Jewell	Ford Cortina	https://www.flickr.com/photos/autohistorian/23233330804/	Attribution 2.0 Generic (CC BY 2.0)
Top Actors	Insomnia Cured Here	Sean Connery	https://www.flickr.com/photos/tom-margie/1544299808	Attribution-ShareAlike 2.0 Generic (CC BY-SA 2.0)

Top Actors	Film Star Vintage	Terence Stamp and Julie Christie	https://www.flickr.com/photos/classicvintage/9488747969/	Attribution 2.0 Generic (CC BY 2.0)
Top Actresses	Pipe Loyola M	Elizabeth Taylor	https://www.flickr.com/photos/solo_antonio/5587360422/	Attribution 2.0 Generic (CC BY 2.0)
Top Actresses	Kate gabrielle	Julie Christie	https://www.flickr.com/photos/slightlyterrific/5379686587/	Attribution 2.0 Generic (CC BY 2.0)
The Beatles	Badreeb pictures	with the beatles	https://www.flickr.com/photos/badgreeb/4202506385/	Attribution-ShareAlike 2.0 Generic (CC BY-SA 2.0)
The Beatles	Kevin Dooley	The Beatles Help	https://www.flickr.com/photos/pagedooley/4663389110/	Attribution 2.0 Generic (CC BY 2.0)
The Beatles	Roger	Abbey Road- The Beatles	https://www.flickr.com/photos/beatlesmaniac11/4191789760/	Attribution 2.0 Generic (CC BY 2.0)
England Win Football World Cup	Karen Horton	england-world-cup-1966-stamp-cunha	https://www.flickr.com/photos/karenhorton/4782400950/	Attribution 2.0 Generic (CC BY 2.0)
The first Concorde Flight	Andrey Korchagin	The first Concorde	https://www.flickr.com/photos/peer_gynt/2958892097/	Attribution-ShareAlike 2.0 Generic (CC BY-SA 2.0)
James Bond Movie	Johan Oomen	DR. NO	https://www.flickr.com/photos/ateam/4218676097/	Attribution-ShareAlike 2.0 Generic (CC BY-SA 2.0)
Ice Lollies	Mike	Raymond Wallbank at the Organ- Relax & Listen	https://www.flickr.com/photos/abaraphobia/5013729447/in/photolist-8D3F6a	Attribution-ShareAlike 2.0 Generic (CC BY-SA 2.0)
Women's Fashioin	Daves_archive1	showrax 1967	https://www.flickr.com/photos/foundin_a_attic/40840055472/	Attribution 2.0 Generic (CC BY 2.0)
Women's Fashioin	IISG	Jackie Kennedy mode	https://www.flickr.com/photos/iisg/6331549562/	Attribution-ShareAlike 2.0 Generic (CC BY-SA 2.0)
Women's Fashioin	Mike	Trip to Lincolnshire	https://www.flickr.com/photos/abaraphobia/11051571553/	Attribution-ShareAlike 2.0 Generic (CC BY-SA 2.0)
Vintage Post Cards from '60s	Mark Crombie	CORNISH POST CARD	https://www.flickr.com/photos/147645911@N08/50626834768/	Public Domain

Vintage Post Cards from '60s	Josh Graciano	Another View of Piccadilly	https://www.flickr.com/photos/newmundane/5570296510/	Attribution-ShareAlike 2.0 Generic (CC BY-SA 2.0)
Vintage Post Cards from '60s	ausdew	CARDIFF CASTLE	https://www.flickr.com/photos/ausdew/43138605595/	Public Domain
Vintage Post Cards from '60s	SludgeG	Hoddesdon postcard, mid 1960s	https://www.flickr.com/photos/sludgeulper/37430886881/	Attribution-ShareAlike 2.0 Generic (CC BY-SA 2.0)
School in the 1960s	SludgeG	Westfields,Chelmsford 1960s	https://www.flickr.com/photos/sludgeulper/2755147351/	Attribution-ShareAlike 2.0 Generic (CC BY-SA 2.0)
City Life	ausdew	Market Street and Cross Street Manchester	https://www.flickr.com/photos/ausdew/47033481274/	Public Domain
City Life	ausdew	SNOW IN LONDON CITY	https://www.flickr.com/photos/ausdew/41035204550/	Public Domain
Families	Daves_archive1	Hoddesdon postcard, mid 1960s	https://www.flickr.com/photos/foundin_a_attic/41207697224/	Attribution 2.0 Generic (CC BY 2.0)
Families	Daves_archive1	lot 1960s uk	https://www.flickr.com/photos/foundin_a_attic/50336319122/	Attribution 2.0 Generic (CC BY 2.0)
Families	Daves_archive1	some uk mixed in	https://www.flickr.com/photos/foundin_a_attic/36351281884/	Attribution 2.0 Generic (CC BY 2.0)
British Comics	ausdew	1962-12-22 BENTLEY SUPERCHARGED 4.5 LITRE - Eagle Comic -	https://www.flickr.com/photos/ausdew/49131091611/	Public Domain
British Comics	ausdew	THE DALESMAN	https://www.flickr.com/photos/ausdew/52116202850/	Public Domain
British Comics	ausdew	SWIFT COMIC 1963-01-05	https://www.flickr.com/photos/ausdew/50204517981/	Public Domain
British Comics	ausdew	1962-04-28 AA	https://www.flickr.com/photos/ausdew/24011662695/	Public Domain

www.ingramcontent.com/pod-product-compliance
Lightning Source LLC
Chambersburg PA
CBHW042047140726
48006CB00020BA/2658